The Total Classroom Management Makeover

Also by Michael Linsin:

The Smart Classroom Management Way
The Happy Teacher Habits
Classroom Management for Art, Music, and PE Teachers
The Classroom Management Secret
Dream Class

The Total Classroom Management Makeover

in 18 short, simple lessons

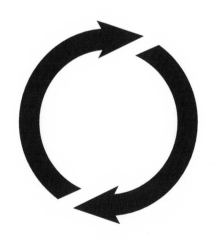

Michael Linsin

JME Publishing
San Diego, California
smartclassroommanagement.com

ISBN: 9781088754320

Almost everything is noise,
and a very few things are exceptionally valuable.

—Greg McKeown, author of *Essentialism*

Contents

Introduction

The Smart Classroom Management website (SCM), which I started in 2009, is made up of hundreds of strategies and is a great resource to many thousands of teachers. But if you want to put together a simple, comprehensive classroom management approach you can count on day after day, it's hard to know where to begin. It's hard to know how all the strategies fit together and which are most important.

When I take over a new class, or if I were to take over your class tomorrow, I would focus on just a few core strategies to transform those students into the kind of happy and well-behaved class that I want to teach. And it is these exact strategies, 18 in all, that you're going to learn in this book.

They're presented as simple dos and don'ts that will bring about the changes in motivation, behavior, and work habits that make for a successful and fulfilling teaching career. They make up a reliable system of classroom management that anyone can do, that works no matter your grade level or where you teach, and that you can feel good about.

The Total Classroom Management Makeover is a condensed shortcut to effective classroom management. It's based on a philosophy that puts the students' academic and social development first, which also happens to be best for you. It's specifically and uniquely designed to create within each student strong intrinsic motivation to listen, learn, and behave.

Most teachers pick and choose their classroom management strategies from dozens of different resources, not knowing that many of them were never meant to be used together. In fact, they often work against each other and make classroom management far more difficult than it needs to be. There are also scores of commonly recommended strategies that may curb misbehavior in the moment, but make things worse over time. They can even harm students and make you feel uncomfortable and manipulative using.

In this book, everything you'll learn is honest, transparent, and best for students long-term. In other words, you can be proud of how you manage your classroom. The strategies are effective individually, but together they're transformative and will only get stronger over time.

Before we get started, I want to mention that I've made each lesson *as simple as possible.* Therefore, you won't find lengthy explanations or advice for specific situations, which have already been covered in my previous books. What you will find is the exact approach I use with every class I teach. It's presented in a way that is easy to understand and easy to know what to do to be an exceptional teacher. The lessons are short and to the point and include only the bare essentials.

My promise to you is that if you earnestly put what you learn into practice, you'll have the hardest-working, best-behaved class in your school. I'm excited to begin and I hope you are too. See you in the first lesson.

Tidy Up

THE FIRST LESSON IS to remove all clutter from your classroom so that when it's empty, it looks simple and spacious. Books, laptops, materials, projects … anything and everything that isn't part of the furniture should be put away or kept neat and tidy. It's important that you exaggerate this orderly look.

You know you're on the right track when everyone who enters your classroom makes a comment about it or tiptoes in like they're visiting a museum. Every parent, teacher, and student should be initially taken aback by your room's appearance. If they're not, then you haven't gone far enough. The idea is to send the message, without saying a word, that excellence is expected; that being part of your classroom is different. This is a powerful strategy that will help establish high standards for everything you do.

Furthermore, research shows that when visual stimuli are chaotic, children tend to behave chaotically. A clutter-filled room is distracting and stressful. It interferes with their sense of safety and well-being. It creates excitability, which is one of the biggest causes of misbehavior. It makes your goal of having a well-behaved class more difficult because every day you must overcome the message of carelessness and mediocrity the visual environment is blasting to your students.

Neatness, on the other hand, brings peace and focus and is consistent with the strategies described in the lessons to follow. It's consistent with the new you and the fresh approach that will greet students every morning and open their eyes to the intrinsic rewards of pursuing excellence.

So throw away the clutter. Get rid of the nonessentials, including any materials you haven't used in the past year. Keep the top of your desk sparse and pleasing to the eye. Ensure your students pick up after themselves, keep their own desks clean, and straighten the furniture before they leave for the day.

Make your classroom stand out in its simplicity and call for excellence. It's a small investment in time, but worth every second. Do this first, make it a daily habit, and everything else you'll learn in this book will more easily click into place.

LESSON 2:

Remove Friction

D ECIDE RIGHT NOW, THIS very moment, to never again use any method that causes friction with students. By friction, I'm referring to anything that causes them to dislike or resent you. This includes sarcasm, lecturing, threatening, glaring, scolding, or any form of intimidation or rejection.

When you take these emotional reactions to misbehavior off the table, when you remove them as possibilities, your entire classroom environment changes. The way your students look at you changes. Their respect for you, confidence in you, and trust in you and your leadership increases tenfold. By just taking the high road, your likability will soar and your students will begin *wanting* to please you and behave for you.

Removing friction gives you the leverage and influence you need to effectively manage even the most challenging classrooms. But here's the thing: You can never go back. You can't for a moment let your guard down and fall into these harmful and stressful behaviors ever again. It's a slippery slope and much easier to get rid of entirely than to just get a little better at it.

The good news is that in time, as you experience the profound change in your students, it will become something you no longer have to think about. It will become just who you are and what you're about every day of the school year.

So make the commitment to never again be the source of friction with any student, no matter how difficult they are, how egregious their behavior, or how frustrated they make you feel. This is an empowering, career-altering decision—and it *is* a decision—and a critical part of your makeover. Much of what's to come hinges on your refusal to use intimidation, coercion, or negativity to try to curb misbehavior or exact your secret revenge. But it's also going to make you a lot freer and happier, especially when you know what to do instead.

LESSON 3:

Stop Rewarding

P UTTING AN END TO rewarding students in exchange for good behavior is one of the best things you can do for them. Token economies, behavior contracts, prize boxes, and other do-this-and-get-that rewards very effectively make your classroom extrinsically motivated. They also weaken, or remove altogether, intrinsic motivation.

You see, when you offer stamps, stickers, free time, or other prizes for good behavior, you're communicating to your students that being polite, respectful, and attentive is work deserving of payment. You're putting a price tag on what is already inherently rewarding, thereby obliterating the intrinsic value of doing what's right and good and valuable to self and others.

Rewarding students makes capturing and keeping their attention, instilling solid work habits, and inspiring a love of learning for its own sake—all the things that keep students on task and away from misbehavior—more difficult. It's also time-consuming and stressful. It makes you feel dirty and manipulative, like you're bribing your students just to get through the day. More importantly, it draws you away from focusing on your primary job: delivering compelling lessons your students will enjoy.

Furthermore, rewards are a short-term fix that weaken over time, so you're constantly upping the ante or changing the reward to satisfy your now bored and jaded class. Worst of all, research shows that they can even embolden unethical behavior like cheating and cutting corners. An extrinsically motivated class is usually one that isn't very nice to each other. Instead, it's often selfish and entitled.

Take the plunge and throw out the rewards, every last one. Don't allow yourself to even consider them. Despite what your colleagues may be doing, or your school district encourages, refuse to take part in anything that isn't best for your students. Remove that which interferes with your ability to create a special community they'll all enjoy and want to be part of.

Just by making this one change, this one simple omission, your students will be a lot happier. They'll work harder. They'll behave consistently better. They'll become more altruistic—true classmates and friends to one and all. It will also make your life a lot easier and free you to start building genuine love for being in your class, which is the greatest reward you could offer.

Note: Utilizing daily points as a form of academic feedback and assessment, which I recommend as part of an effective classroom management plan for high school teachers, is perfectly okay and not considered an extrinsic reward.

LESSON 4:

Stop Convincing

STOP TRYING TO CONVINCE your students to behave. Stop pulling them aside for pep-talks and counseling sessions. Stop imploring them, guilting them, or trying to manipulate them into behaving. Stop appealing to their sense of right and wrong or forcing them to tell you what you want to hear. Stop bluffing and pleading and hoping that someday they're going to improve.

Because, when you have a convince-mindset, through your words and actions you communicate loud and clear how much their behavior means to you. You let them know how it deeply it affects you, stresses you out, and gets under your skin. And in so doing, you weaken your authority and shift control in the relationship from you to them. You give them the power to make or break your day. You surrender the upper hand, which they'll eagerly take.

Now, this isn't something students do deliberately. They're not plotting to usurp your authority. It's just human nature. Where there is a void in leadership—which is what you're doing when you try to persuade better behavior—your students will fill it. And if the opening is large enough, they'll wrest control of the classroom right out of your hands.

Trying to convince students to behave is one of the most common methods of classroom management. I see it in virtually every classroom I visit. It's also an incredibly stressful way to go about your day. If I had to rely on my body language, tone of voice, and creative use of words to somehow coax students into behaving, I wouldn't get out of bed in the morning. I certainly wouldn't be a teacher.

So what's the alternative? See you in the next lesson.

LESSON 5:

Have A Plan

INSTEAD OF TRYING TO intimidate, bribe, or convince students into behaving, you're going to rely exclusively on a classroom management plan. A classroom management plan has two purposes only. The first is to hold students accountable for disruption or disrespect without causing friction in the relationship. The second is to protect every student's right to learn and enjoy school. That's it.

An effective plan consists of a set of rules that cover every possible misbehavior and a set of consequences that matter to students. The plans I recommend, one for elementary and lower middle school teachers and one for high school and upper middle school teachers, are available for purchase and immediate download at smartclassroommanagement.com.

Both plans are proven to work in the most challenging teaching situations imaginable, as well as with the most difficult students.

However, I want to emphasize that there is no magic in the rules and consequences that I recommend. You can certainly come up with your own plan to suit your needs. There are free articles on the SCM website to help you do just that. The magic isn't in the plan itself. It's in your consistency following the plan and your ability to make your consequences matter to students.

My promise to you is that if you follow the advice contained in these lessons, including the previous three, which were simply about what not to do, your consequences *will* matter to your students, and they'll matter to them greatly. After 30 years of teaching many thousands of students in every grade level from kindergarten to seniors in high school, I feel as strongly about this as anything I've ever written.

In most classrooms, the experience of being a member of the class in good standing and the experience of having a consequence feels about the same—which is why the consequences are ineffective. Essentially, what we're doing in this book is learning simple but very powerful ways to widen this gap in experience so your students will like and respect you and being in your classroom so much that they won't want to have anything to do with your consequences.

This is what's known as having leverage. And it's one of the greatest feelings in teaching. When you know that even a gentle warning is enough to stop misbehavior in its tracks, your confidence skyrockets and you have everything you need to be the exceptional teacher you desire.

As mentioned at the top, the wonderful thing about relying on a classroom management plan rather than trying to intimidate, bribe, or convince students is that it's so much less stressful. You'll always know exactly what to do in response to every misbehavior. You'll also have a clear conscience, free from guilt, worry, or fear, knowing that you're managing your classroom in a way that is fair and best for your students.

Finally, letting your plan do the dirty work will free to enjoy your relationships with students. It will free you to teach great lessons, uninterrupted, which in turn makes your plan that much stronger. The next three lessons will cover how to implement your classroom management plan in a way that is most effective.

LESSON 6:

Lay It Out

WHETHER YOU'RE JUST BEGINNING the school year or you want to start over and gain control mid-year, you're going to lay out your classroom management plan in its entirety for your students. You're going to get everything out in the open, letting them know exactly, step by step, what will happen if they misbehave. You do this so there are no surprises or misunderstandings down the line. If they choose to misbehave, they'll know beyond a doubt what the process will be.

This is key to getting them to take responsibility and resolve not to make the same mistakes again. It's also comforting to them to know precisely where your boundary lines are, and that they're fixed and non-negotiable. It allows your students to relax, breathe easy, and focus their energy on learning and enjoying school.

You put yourself on record by explaining your role in enforcing your classroom management plan, and you get your students on record for understanding it. To do this, you must define your plan in minute detail, so they know exactly where the line is and whether or not they've crossed it. This alone, which few teachers do in a complete way, is a powerful deterrent—because it makes every misbehavior a conscious choice rather than an impulsive act.

The younger your students are, the more you need to model your plan—from what breaking each rule looks like to what you will do in response to how they are to take themselves to time-out. But even with high school students, although you may not need to model so explicitly, you'll still need to explain exactly what words you'll use when you approach them and what they mean, as well as how *they* should respond.

By laying it all out ahead of time, you also avoid arguing, complaining, and confusion. You avoid angry phone calls and emails from parents—who you'll also want to put on record by signing your beginning of the year syllabus or informational packet that includes your classroom management plan.

Most importantly, though, by teaching your plan in detail you avoid hurt feelings, resentment, or blaming you for the consequence. Because of your transparency and unwillingness to add to your consequences through lectures, talking-tos, and the like, responsibility for misbehavior will fall completely—100%—on their shoulders, where it belongs and with none of it sticking to you.

So whether it's the beginning of the year or you're starting over midyear, lay it all out. Leave nothing uncovered and nothing to chance. Put everyone on record. And your classroom management plan will start working as it should.

LESSON 7:

Make A Promise

AFTER CONFIRMING THAT YOUR students understand your classroom management plan, you're going to make a very important and public promise to follow it exactly as it was taught. When you put yourself, your integrity, and your trustworthiness on the line by making such a promise to your students, it becomes far easier to follow through. It raises the stakes and puts just enough pressure on you to do what you say you're going to do. In other words, it's a strategy that ensures your consistency.

This is important for three reasons. First, if you don't follow your plan as written, if you enforce consequences based on your mood, the severity of the misbehavior, or who is doing the misbehaving, then your students aren't going to trust you. They will, however, resent you and argue with you at every turn. *Why did Karla get away with leaving her seat without permission and I didn't?* Why indeed? Building influential relationships then, which is a key principle of this book, becomes impossible, especially with your most challenging students.

The second reason is that when there is a price to pay every time a rule is broken, when there is surefire accountability, then misbehavior tends to disappear— especially when combined with an appreciation of you and a love for being in your class, which we'll cover in detail in upcoming lessons.

The third reason is that in absence of every-single-time consistency, you'll more than likely fall into bad habits like glaring, threatening, raising your voice, and other friction-creating behaviors. In classrooms where the teacher is inconsistent, you'll find anger, confrontation, and negative methods nearly 100% of the time.

Just say, "I promise to follow this classroom management plan exactly how it's written and was taught to you." And then do it. Put yourself on the line. Go all in and you'll never be viewed as wishy-washy, weak, or untrustworthy by students again. Instead, you'll be admired as a strong, confident leader they can believe in.

LESSON 8:

Supervise

A COMMON CONCERN TEACHERS HAVE about consistency is: What happens if you don't see the misbehavior? You turn your back, for example, and one student pushes another. How can you be consistent when this happens?

Well, a couple things. First, this type of scenario is far more likely to happen when your students view you as a pushover, as someone who only kinda-sorta holds students accountable. Simply by defining your rules so there is no doubt what is and isn't okay, and following through every time you witness misbehavior, your students will be far less likely to misbehave behind your back. Add to it their newfound respect for you and enjoyment of the class, and the odds become even smaller.

Having said that, it's your job to see misbehavior, as well as everything else in your classroom. The key here is positioning—keeping students in front of you—and keen observation, which we'll cover in an upcoming lesson. If you're distracted and doing last-minute preparation, or you're rushing around trying to help one student after the next, then you're going to give a green light to misbehavior. And you *will* be viewed as a pushover.

One of the biggest deterrents to misbehavior is when every student in the class knows that the teacher, who always follows through, is watching. It's best to think of your role in enforcing rules and consequences as a referee. You keep yourself in position to witness the action, and you call 'em like you see 'em—calmly, unemotionally, even robotically. Then you move on as if nothing happened.

LESSON 9:

Be Pleasant

|N TEACHING CIRCLES, THERE is a lot of talk about how best to build rapport. And for good reason. Having a positive relationship with students makes everything easier and a lot more fun. It also plays a big role in creating an experience your students enjoy being part of, which in turn makes your rules and consequences matter to them.

Conventional wisdom says that building rapport is something you need to work at, that there are strategies you need to employ to create a strong bond with your class. But the truth is, the harder you try, the more you attempt to engage students in conversation and get to know them better, the more you'll end up pushing them away. Because, when you force it, the relationship can become awkward and uncomfortable for students.

Sadly, if you're unaware of this phenomenon, then you'll struggle with building influential rapport and not know why. This will crush your confidence and give you the false belief that you don't have the charisma or gift of gab that you think you need.

So what's the solution? Well, by simply following the previous eight lessons, by refusing to create friction and by consistently protecting your students' right to learn and enjoy school, you're miles ahead of most teachers. By those virtues alone, your students are going to trust and respect you.

But there is one other thing you can do that will draw students *to* you and cause them to want to get to know *you* better. And when students are drawn to you, when they want to interact with you and ask questions about you and spend time with you, then the relationship becomes natural and easy.

This kind of effortless rapport, where students surround you after class and you freely laugh and banter with them, happens automatically when you're simply and consistently pleasant. If you merely refrain from scolding, lecturing, threatening, and creating friction, and instead are just nice and friendly, you'll never have to worry about building relationships again. *They* will come to you.

It's important to mention that relying on your classroom management plan is what enables you to express your personality and enjoy being around your students. If you're not following your plan, then you're likely to fall into bad habits and behaviors that sabotage, often severely, your ability to build relationships.

One more thing: This level of rapport gives you tremendous power and leverage to influence behavior. In other words, your students will go to great lengths not to disappoint you or disrupt your class. Instead, they'll want to please you, listen to you, and behave for you. In the next lesson, I'm going to show you a way to ensure that you're able to maintain you're pleasant demeanor throughout every day of the school year.

LESSON 10:

Decide

'VE HAD THE OPPORTUNITY to visit a lot of classrooms over the years, and there is one characteristic that is always present in those rooms where the teacher is struggling with behavior. It's excitability. Excitability is a feeling of nervous tension that permeates the classroom. There is a buzz of energy, agitation, and restlessness that if you look closely you can see on the students' faces and in their body language. They look as if they're going to start climbing the walls.

Excitability is something an outsider can feel immediately upon walking in the door. It gives me the heebie-jeebies and is the first clue that the teacher is in need of a lot of help. What's interesting, however, is that while visitors can feel it plainly, the teacher very often cannot. They've either grown accustomed to the stress and unease or they assume that it's just part of teaching. Well, it's not.

Now, much of what we've covered so far goes a long way toward keeping your classroom calm and peaceful. But there is one thing in particular that has the greatest effect on excitability. It's something you must fix if you are to create the teaching experience you really desire. What is it? It's your temperament.

Nothing sweeps excitability out of the classroom, as well as the misbehavior that comes with it, more effectively than a calm leader. Again, the previous nine lessons are going to automatically make you calmer. Also, just knowing how important it is can be helpful.

But I recommend a technique that is proven to keep you as serene as a mountain lake. Even if you're normally a nervous or anxious person, it will allow you to maintain that rapport-building pleasantness all day long.

The way it works is that every morning before your students arrive you're going to shut your classroom door and take a moment to just breathe and relax. Then you're going to close your eyes and make a very important and conscious decision. You're going to decide that no matter what happens that day—even if a herd of water buffaloes comes charging through your door—you're going to keep your cool inside and out. You're not going to allow yourself to feel or behave in any other way. And that's it. That's the entire strategy.

Now, I realize that it seems almost too simple. It seems as if it couldn't possibly work, but it's amazing how effective it is. It's amazing how different you'll feel and how much easier you'll be able to keep your composure. In time, as your students become more comfortable and happy being part of your class, and as you experience how wonderful it feels, it will become something you no longer have to think about. It will become your teaching persona, just the way you go about your day.

So make that decision, every morning, to keep a calm, even keel throughout the day. This way, you'll be able to maintain your pleasant demeanor, build rapport effortlessly, and keep excitability from entering your classroom ever again.

Teach In Detail

ONE OF THE SECRETS to good classroom management, and good teaching for that matter, is to teach everything you want your students to be able to do in extreme detail. It doesn't matter if you're teaching a routine, an academic lesson, or how you want your students to collect science materials.

Teachers who struggle with misbehavior and poor listening tend to gloss over details and rush through lessons. They do this because they fear that their students are going to get bored and start misbehaving. But the opposite is true. Details *are* interesting. Details are compelling and help students stay focused. They also set them up for success by showing them exactly what they need to do to meet your standards.

For elementary teachers, this will involve a lot of modeling. You'll want to model all new learning. The only thing you won't model are routines you do every day that your students have already proven they can perform. But for everything else, you'll put yourself in their shoes, pretending to be an actual student in your class, and show them precisely what you expect.

If you're a high school teacher, depending on your grade level, you can substitute much of the modeling for explanation and pantomiming in place what you expect. But the key is to teach everything you want them to do, perform, or accomplish in exacting detail.

Clarity is king, so leave no stone unturned and no question unanswered. Again, detail is interesting. It pulls students deeper into your lessons. It prepares them for independent work that is truly independent. Being a stickler for the nitty-gritty is a trait that all great teachers share. It's a secret that makes the art of teaching more fun, effective, and impactful. We're going to build upon this idea in the next several lessons.

LESSON 12:

Take Your Time

A S YOU'RE FOCUSING ON the details, it's important that you take your time, that you're not in a hurry to check objectives off your list or squeeze as many things as you can into one lesson. Ironically, to go faster, to progress swiftly through your curriculum, you must slow down and teach more thoroughly—because excellence transfers from one lesson to the next, and so do listening and work habits. When you teach it right the first time, you never have to reteach and you're continually building upon stronger and stronger habits.

Time on task increases, learning increases, confusion all but disappears, and each objective takes less and less time to cover as the year goes on. Soon, you'll be flying through the curriculum—although you're still taking your time from moment to moment.

The idea is to do one thing well at a time, to teach it right, and then have your students prove they understand and can perform independently. Then move on to the next thing and do that well. And so on. Never give mediocrity or shoddy work a foothold. Create good, precise habits from the start and never, ever let them slide.

Teachers who struggle tend to rush students off to perform routines, transitions, or independent work without making sure they know exactly what's expected—which very effectively grooves the habit of doing things poorly, infecting every subsequent lesson and activity. Misbehavior then, predictably, comes into play and increases in both frequency and severity. Learning suffers and it feels like you're scrambling to catch up. Stress and tension also enter the equation, and unless you slow down and refocus your class on detailed excellence, you'll never regain control.

So take your time. Keep your students with you, in the present moment. Teach in detail, check thoroughly for understanding, and guide your class from one success to the next all day long.

Praise

T HE SUCCESS THAT STEMS from teaching in detail and taking your time provides ample opportunity to give your students genuine praise. This is important because praise, as long as it's based on true accomplishment, is your most effective means of providing feedback. It tells students in a very clear way that they're on the right track, which *keeps* them on the right track.

Now, it's important to mention that false praise—that is, praise based on what are common expectations—will only confuse them, weaken their motivation, and lower the bar on what is considered quality work.

So what is true accomplishment and therefore worthy of your praise? Any new learning done correctly or any effort or performance that goes beyond what your class or individual students have done before. This means that anything previously taught and successfully learned becomes an expectation. Good behavior, too, is an expectation. The only time you'll praise behavior is if a student makes marked improvement over time—say two weeks, at the least.

Keeping your praise worthy and genuine will make your words meaningful to students. It will make your words precious to them; words their itching ears long to hear. So when they do receive praise from you, they'll know that it's real and well earned. Which feels great, especially because it's coming from someone they look up to, admire, and have a treasured relationship with.

When you guide your students from and through one successful lesson to the next, and you're praising them along the way (for new learning), success becomes a way of life in your classroom. It's important to note that your praise doesn't have to be loud, excessive, or over-the-top. Sometimes the subtlest word or nod of the head is the most powerful thing you can do.

To sum up, if you witness new learning, improved skill, better performance, or greater effort, then give them positive feedback. If it's expected, though, something they already know or have proven they can do, then hold your tongue—or just say thank you.

LESSON 14:

Teach One Thing

CONTINUING THE THEME OF teaching in detail, taking your time, and providing feedback through praise, it's important that you only focus on one, clear objective at a time. Never begin any instruction or activity unless you have a goal for what you want your students to be able to do.

A clear-cut objective keeps you on target. I can't emphasize this enough. It keeps your instruction, your activities, your stories, modeling segments, and directions aligned and focused. It ensures that your students know what you expect of them.

Teachers who struggle with classroom management are often all over the place with their instruction. They talk too much and go off on tangents. They add unnecessary fluff and asides that draw students away from their objective, which is rarely clear to begin with. The result is that their lessons are uninteresting. The students are lost and bored. They daydream, become restless, and are now primed to misbehave.

To keep them attentive and on-task, you must have a singular goal you're shooting for, an objective you want to accomplish. This doesn't mean that your lessons won't include skills and objectives learned in previous lessons. It doesn't mean that they won't be challenging or contain multiple steps. It means that your objective will be abundantly clear to every student. So clear, in fact, that they should be able to tell you at any time what that objective is and why they're doing what they're doing. This keeps students interested, accountable, filled with purpose, and out of trouble.

While planning, when you look through your resources to design a lesson, pick out only one thing to focus on and cut out the rest. Narrow in, simplify, and deepen. Take your time and teach the heck out it. Now is the time to show your passion for making your subject come alive for your students. Let loose and enjoy the *performance* of teaching.

Just be sure that there is no question, no misunderstanding, no doubt what you want your students to be able to do, create, perform, or accomplish. Great instruction is one of your biggest responsibilities—second only to the safety of your students. In the next lesson, we're going to talk about your students and their number one responsibility.

LESSON 15:

Shift Responsibility

THE PREVIOUS FOUR LESSONS—EXTREME detail, taking your time, worthy praise, and having one objective—were all about teaching effective lessons, whether strictly academic or classroom policies and routines. They were about keeping students on task and far away from misbehavior. They were about preparing them for the next step, which is shifting responsibility for learning over to them.

Every lesson you teach should have a period of time for your students to practice independently whatever you've taught them. That is, without additional help from you. This could be work they do individually or in groups, but it is done *entirely* on their own.

Shifting responsibility in total over to them will increase learning, improve maturity, and motivate your students intrinsically more than anything else you can do.

Teachers who micromanage, who are quick to kneel down and reteach individual students what was taught to the entire class minutes before, struggle mightily with neediness, poor work habits, inattentiveness, and the misbehavior that comes with it.

You see, when you do for students what they can do for themselves, when you prod and help and hint them along, you create a culture of learned helplessness. You create a class full of students who are immature, dependent, and distracted and have little confidence in their abilities. Therefore, predictably, instead of getting down to work, they misbehave. They make excuses. They slide low in their seats and stare at the walls.

To wean them off the false belief that they need you, teach great lessons and then be very wary about helping. Instead, keep your distance and say, "I know you can do it," "I believe in you," or simply, "You don't need my help."

In time, this day-after-day, thrum-beat message that they can and will do the work, results in tenacious independence. It improves listening and attentiveness. It builds confidence and endurance. It imbues them with grit and toughness and increases academic achievement tenfold. As for what you're to do during this time, on to the next lesson.

LESSON 16:

Observe

S HIFTING RESPONSIBILITY IN FULL over
to students in the form of independent or group
work after teaching an effective lesson frees you
to observe your class—which, frankly, is something
that most teachers just don't do. They're either too busy
helping students one after the other or scurrying about
getting ready for the next activity.

But observation is critical because it allows you to
really get to know your class and their strengths and
weaknesses. It helps you adjust your instruction the following day to better meet their needs. Furthermore, just
knowing that you're watching, and that you always follow
through, is a powerful deterrent against misbehavior.

True observation is a rarity in most classrooms, where you'll find students taking advantage of the poor supervision by chatting, goofing around, interrupting learning, and so on.

Practically, good observation entails fading into the background. You may, at times, stand in one place, a few yards back, so you're not in any way a distraction to your students. At other times you may be silently moving about the room looking over shoulders—but again, from a distance at which they won't notice you.

Uninterrupted independent work is key to their academic development. Your students have to be given a chance to wrestle with the challenges you place before them. Although through clear and detailed lessons we set our students up for success, a bit of struggle with the content is a good thing. It's only when we notice sustained frustration that cues us to step in with a word of encouragement or a subtle hint. Otherwise, we leave our students alone.

Now, if you're reading this book midyear, you may want to start slow, with just a few minutes of truly independent work. You can then build on this time until you get to the point where you must reluctantly stop them from working in order to move on to the next subject or transition.

Teach great lessons with a singular objective, check thoroughly for understanding, and answer every question they have beforehand. Make them prove they get it.

Provide everything they need to succeed and then turn them loose to discuss the book, perform the experiment, or solve for x while you look on from afar.

LESSON 17:

Never Lose Control

ONCE YOU MAKEOVER YOUR classroom and implement each of the previous lessons, improvement will come fast. You should notice within the first couple of days that things are a lot different than what you've experienced in the past. Behavior, maturity, and independence in particular should all be substantially improved.

However, at some point, inevitably, you're going to be faced with the prospect of more than one student misbehaving at the same time, which is nothing to be overly concerned about. Eventually, it will be a rare occurrence, but in the beginning it's not unusual to be tested to see if the new you is for real. And when you are, it will prompt a particular response, or rule of thumb, I want you to follow.

When you witness a few students misbehaving concurrently, say two or three, four at the most, you're going to follow your classroom management plan as normal. You're going to calmly enforce a consequence and then turn and be on your way. If, however, more than a few students are misbehaving, in which case it's usually a lot more, then it's a sign that you need to back up and reteach whatever it was you were doing when the misbehavior began.

In other words, it's on you. Either you weren't detailed enough in your instruction and expectations or you were moving too fast. Now, it's important to point out that this can also happen if you've been less than consistent. If you haven't been following your plan as it's written, then at some point your students are going to ignore your directions and do as they please. If this is the case, then stop immediately, reteach your plan, and make a new promise to follow it.

The idea is to start over right away, before things start going south. At the first sign that the train is going off the rails, *do not move on* under any circumstance. Back up. Reassert your expectations. Model and practice as needed. Nip misbehavior and unruliness in the bud before it gets a toehold. Send the message that things really have changed, that you will not accept anything less than their best. This will ensure that you'll never lose control again.

LESSON 18:

Be Great

THE PREVIOUS 17 LESSONS, when knitted together, will cause your students to love being part of your class—the greatest reward you could ever offer—and to *want* to listen, learn, and behave for you. They'll create strong, intrinsic motivation naturally and all but eliminate stress from your teaching life.

Thousands of teachers have put these same strategies into practice, and are now enjoying uncommon classroom management and teaching success.

But you have to go all in. You have to decide to become great at these few things. It's not a lot, and anyone can do it, but picking and choosing or going halfway, isn't going to do. Being average isn't going to do.

So don't settle. Don't give in. Don't fall back into bad habits. Take the knowledge you've learned and work at it. Improve every day. Turn it into a skill that becomes second nature, one that will allow you to make an enduring impact on your students, your community, and the wider world.

You'll be forever changed, I promise, and so will your students.

Review

What follows is a quick review of the book, so you can have a refresher at your fingertips whenever you need it.

1. Tidy up your classroom to send the message that excellence is expected.

2. Remove all friction to build automatic trust, respect, and likability.

3. Stop rewarding exchange for good behavior in favor of intrinsic motivation.

4. Stop trying to convince your students to behave, which weakens your authority and shifts control to them.

5. Have a classroom management plan that protects your students' right to learn and enjoy school.

6. Lay everything out up front so there is no misunderstanding about where your boundary lines are and what happens if they're crossed.

7. Make a promise to follow your classroom management plan exactly as it's written.

8. Position yourself to supervise closely and fulfill your promise to be every-single-time consistent.

9. Be pleasant from morning bell to dismissal to build effortless rapport, leverage, and influence.

10. Decide every morning to be calm no matter what happens in order to maintain your pleasant demeanor and eliminate excitability.

11. Teach in extreme detail, which is interesting to students and sets them up for success.

12. Take your time so your students are clear about what you expect, and you can guide them from one success to the next.

13. Give worthy praise to provide the feedback your students need to keep improving.

14. Focus on one objective at a time to keep your students interested, on-task, and far from misbehavior.

15. Shift responsibility in full over to your students, which improves learning, maturity, and independence.

16. Observe from afar to really get to know your class and provide a strong deterrent against misbehavior.

17. If a few students misbehave, follow your plan as normal. If it's more than a few, it's on you and you must back up and reteach.

18. Be great at these few things and your students will be intrinsically motivated to listen, learn, and behave.

Note: If you'd like to dig deeper into the whys and hows of any of the topics presented in this book, or learn how to implement dozens of supporting strategies, please visit smartclassroommanagement.com.